Women Entrepreneurs in the Modern World

C. P. Kumar
Reiki Healer & Author
Roorkee - 247667, India

Disclaimer

While every effort has been made to ensure the accuracy and completeness of the content in this book, the author cannot guarantee that the information contained herein is error-free, up-to-date, or suitable for every individual circumstance.

The author shall not be held liable or responsible for any errors or omissions in the content of the book, nor for any damages, or losses that may arise from any actions taken based upon the suggestions or contents presented in the book.

Readers are advised to use their own judgment and discretion in applying the information provided in this book, and to consult with qualified professionals before taking any action based on the contents of this book. The author disclaims any and all liability or responsibility for any actions taken or not taken based on the information contained in this book.

DEDICATION

To all the women who dared to dream, who defied convention, and who forged their paths in the world of entrepreneurship.

Your resilience, determination, and unwavering spirit have illuminated the way for generations to come.

May this book serve as a tribute to your journey, an acknowledgment of your triumphs, and a testament to the transformative power of women in business.

In admiration and gratitude, this book is dedicated to you.

C. P. Kumar

CONTENTS

PREFACE

In the dynamic landscape of entrepreneurship, women have long been at the forefront of innovation, resilience, and change. Their journeys, marked by challenges, triumphs, and relentless pursuit of their dreams, have shaped industries, economies, and societies worldwide. This book, "Women Entrepreneurs in the Modern World", delves into the multifaceted realm of women's entrepreneurship, offering insights, inspiration, and invaluable lessons drawn from diverse experiences across the globe.

Within these pages lie narratives that traverse time and geography, from historical perspectives illuminating the roots of women's entrepreneurial endeavors to futuristic visions shaping the landscape of tomorrow. Through a comprehensive exploration of themes, challenges, and opportunities, this book embarks on a journey to unravel the complexities and celebrate the triumphs of women in entrepreneurship.

The chapters within this book explore the intricacies of women's entrepreneurship, from understanding the historical contexts that have shaped and defined their roles to navigating the contemporary challenges and seizing the abundant opportunities available today.

As we journey through these pages, we confront the realities of challenges and opportunities that define the entrepreneurial landscape for women. From the intricacies of leadership and management styles to the disruptive forces of innovation and the digital frontier, each section offers a nuanced perspective on the evolving dynamics of women in business.

Navigating male-dominated industries and building robust support networks emerge as essential strategies in overcoming barriers and fostering resilience. Balancing work and life becomes not just a personal endeavor but a societal imperative for sustainable success.

Addressing disparities in access to capital and advocating for policy changes become pivotal points of intervention, fostering an enabling environment for women entrepreneurs to thrive.

As we delve deeper, the narrative expands to encompass the broader implications of women's entrepreneurship, from driving social impact and sustainability to exploring global perspectives and overcoming personal hurdles such as impostor syndrome.

Failure and resilience emerge as rites of passage, transforming setbacks into stepping stones toward growth and empowerment. Finally, we cast our gaze toward the horizon, contemplating the future of women entrepreneurship and the boundless possibilities that await.

In this anthology of stories, insights, and reflections, we invite you to embark on a transformative journey - a journey that celebrates the indomitable spirit of women entrepreneurs and heralds a future where barriers dissolve, opportunities flourish, and voices resonate with purpose.

May this book serve as a beacon of inspiration, empowerment, and advocacy, illuminating pathways to progress and prosperity for women entrepreneurs in the modern world.

Welcome to the journey.

C. P. Kumar
Reiki Healer & Author
Former Scientist 'G', National Institute of Hydrology
Roorkee - 247667, India
Web: https://www.angelfire.com/nh/cpkumar/virgo.html

Chapter 1. Historical Perspectives

Introduction

In the modern world, the narrative of entrepreneurship has predominantly been crafted around the achievements and innovations of men. However, beneath the surface lies a rich tapestry of women who have been instrumental in shaping economies, industries, and societies through their entrepreneurial endeavors. Understanding the historical context and evolution of women in entrepreneurship provides a foundational understanding of the challenges they have faced, the barriers they have overcome, and the strides they have made in claiming their place in the business world.

Ancient Roots: Women as Economic Agents

The history of women in entrepreneurship dates back to ancient civilizations where women played pivotal roles as economic agents. In societies such as ancient Egypt, Mesopotamia, and China, women engaged in various entrepreneurial activities, including trade, craftwork, and agriculture. Despite societal norms that often relegated them to domestic spheres, women seized opportunities to participate in commerce and enterprise, albeit within the constraints of patriarchal systems.

Medieval Guilds and Urban Economies

During the medieval period (5th to the 15th century), women's participation in entrepreneurship became more structured within the framework of guilds (associations of craftsmen and merchants) and urban economies. While men dominated guilds and formal trade associations, women carved out niches in sectors such as textiles, brewing, and medicine. The rise of urban centers provided women with avenues for economic autonomy, although their access to resources and legal rights remained limited compared to their male counterparts.

Industrial Revolution

The Industrial Revolution marked a turning point in the history of women in entrepreneurship. As economies transitioned from agrarian to industrial, new opportunities emerged for women to venture into manufacturing, retail, and service industries. Women entrepreneurs played crucial roles in cottage industries, textile mills, and small-scale enterprises, contributing to the economic transformation of societies. However, gender norms and discriminatory practices persisted, relegating many women to low-paying jobs and informal sectors.

Suffrage Movement and Women's Empowerment

The late 19th and early 20th centuries witnessed the rise of the suffrage movement and women's empowerment campaigns, laying the groundwork for greater female participation in entrepreneurship. The suffrage movement was a social and political campaign aimed at securing voting rights for women. Suffragists advocated for equal political participation and representation for women.

As women gained political and social rights, they also sought economic independence and self-reliance. Pioneers such as Madam C. J. Walker, the first female self-made millionaire in the United States, challenged racial and gender barriers to build successful businesses and empower other women of color.

World Wars and Economic Mobilization

The tumultuous periods of World War I and World War II brought about significant shifts in women's roles in entrepreneurship. With men deployed in military service, women stepped into the workforce en masse, assuming leadership positions in factories, businesses, and government agencies. The war efforts showcased women's capacity for innovation, adaptability, and managerial skills, paving the way for post-war economic opportunities and policy reforms that recognized women's contributions to the economy.

Post-War Boom and Corporate Glass Ceilings

The post-war economic boom of the mid-20th century witnessed the rise of corporate America and the proliferation of consumer culture. While women made strides in entering professional fields and managerial roles, they encountered persistent barriers to advancement, commonly referred to as the "glass ceiling". Despite achieving higher levels of education and expertise, women faced systemic discrimination and limited access to capital, networks, and mentorship opportunities within male-dominated corporate structures.

Feminist Movements and Entrepreneurial Resurgence

The feminist movements of the late 20th century catalyzed a resurgence of women in entrepreneurship, challenging traditional gender norms and advocating for equal rights and opportunities in the business world. Grassroots initiatives, networking forums, and support networks provided women entrepreneurs with platforms to share experiences, exchange resources, and mobilize for policy reforms. The proliferation of digital technologies and e-commerce platforms further democratized access to markets and facilitated the rise of women-led startups and ventures.

Globalization and Transnational Entrepreneurship

In the era of globalization, women entrepreneurs have increasingly engaged in transnational ventures, leveraging digital technologies, cross-border networks, and global supply chains to expand their reach and impact. From micro-enterprises (small businesses characterized by their size, typically employing a small number of people and often operated by a single individual or a small team) in developing countries to multinational corporations led by women CEOs, entrepreneurship has become a powerful vehicle for economic empowerment, social mobility, and sustainable development on a global scale. However, disparities in access to resources, education, and infrastructure persist, particularly for women in marginalized communities and conflict-affected regions.

Contemporary Challenges and Opportunities

In the 21st century, women continue to confront a myriad of challenges and barriers in entrepreneurship, ranging from gender bias and stereotype threat to unequal access to funding and *venture capital*. Despite these obstacles, women entrepreneurs have demonstrated resilience, creativity, and leadership in diverse sectors such as technology, healthcare, finance, and social enterprise. Initiatives aimed at promoting women's entrepreneurship, including mentorship programs, *incubators*, and policy reforms, have gained momentum, signaling a growing recognition of the economic and social dividends of gender equality and inclusion.

Venture capital is a form of private equity investment that provides funding to high-potential startups and small businesses in exchange for equity ownership, aiming to support their growth and innovation.

Incubators are organizations or programs that support the development and growth of early-stage startups and entrepreneurs by providing resources, mentorship, networking opportunities, and sometimes funding, typically in exchange for equity or fees. They offer a supportive environment to help startups refine their business models, access expertise, and accelerate their growth trajectory.

Conclusion: Toward a More Inclusive Future

The historical perspectives of women in entrepreneurship underscore the enduring legacy of resilience, resourcefulness, and innovation in the face of adversity. As we navigate the complexities of the modern business landscape, it is imperative to acknowledge the contributions and challenges of women entrepreneurs and strive for a more inclusive and equitable future. By dismantling systemic barriers, fostering supportive ecosystems, and amplifying diverse voices and narratives, we can unlock the full potential of women as catalysts for economic growth, innovation, and social change in the modern world.

Chapter 2. Challenges and Opportunities

Introduction

In the dynamic landscape of entrepreneurship, women have been making remarkable strides, redefining norms, and breaking barriers. However, their journey is not without challenges. In this article, we delve into the multifaceted realm of women entrepreneurship, exploring the hurdles they encounter and the myriad of opportunities awaiting their exploration.

The entrepreneurial realm has long been dominated by men, but the tide is changing. Women entrepreneurs are increasingly stepping into the spotlight, bringing fresh perspectives, innovative ideas, and unwavering determination to the table. Despite their undeniable potential, women continue to face a myriad of challenges on their path to success.

Challenges on the Horizon

1. Gender Bias and Stereotypes

One of the most pervasive challenges faced by women entrepreneurs is gender bias and stereotypes deeply ingrained in societal structures. From seeking funding to navigating professional networks, women often encounter prejudice and skepticism based solely on their gender. These biases can undermine confidence, limit opportunities, and impede growth potential.

2. Access to Funding and Resources

Access to capital remains a significant obstacle for women entrepreneurs. Studies reveal that female-led startups receive a disproportionately smaller share of venture capital funding compared to their male counterparts. Limited access to financial resources constrains expansion plans, stifles innovation, and perpetuates the cycle of inequality within the entrepreneurial ecosystem.

3. Work-Life Balance Struggles

Balancing the demands of entrepreneurship with familial responsibilities poses a formidable challenge for many women. The expectation to excel both professionally and personally often leads to feelings of guilt, burnout, and self-doubt. Striking a harmonious equilibrium between work and life commitments requires resilience, support systems, and the flexibility to adapt to evolving priorities.

4. Lack of Mentorship and Networking Opportunities

Mentorship and networking play pivotal roles in entrepreneurial success, yet women often encounter barriers in accessing these invaluable resources. Limited representation of female mentors and leaders within established networks further exacerbates the disparity. The absence of mentorship deprives aspiring women entrepreneurs of guidance, insights, and the essential support needed to navigate the intricate pathways of business ownership.

Opportunities on the Horizon

Amidst the challenges, women entrepreneurs are harnessing a myriad of opportunities to thrive, innovate, and leave an indelible mark on the entrepreneurial landscape.

1. Rise of Women-Centric Initiatives

The emergence of women-centric initiatives, incubators, and *accelerators* signifies a burgeoning movement towards fostering inclusivity and empowerment within the entrepreneurial sphere. These platforms provide tailored support, mentorship, and resources specifically designed to address the unique challenges faced by women entrepreneurs, propelling them towards sustainable growth and success.

Accelerators are programs or organizations that support early-stage startups by providing mentorship, resources, networking opportunities, and sometimes funding in exchange for equity. Unlike incubators, accelerators typically have a fixed duration, often lasting several months, during which startups receive intensive support to rapidly grow their businesses and prepare for further investment or market entry.

2. Embracing Technology and Digital Innovation

Technology has emerged as a powerful equalizer, leveling the playing field and opening doors to new possibilities for women entrepreneurs. From e-commerce platforms to digital marketing strategies, technology enables women to reach global audiences, streamline operations, and scale their ventures with unprecedented efficiency. Embracing digital innovation empowers women to transcend geographical boundaries, tap into diverse markets, and capitalize on emerging trends in the digital economy.

3. Cultivating Collaborative Communities

The power of collaboration and community cannot be overstated in the entrepreneurial journey. Women entrepreneurs are forging alliances, building networks, and creating collaborative communities that celebrate diversity, foster creativity, and amplify collective voices. By nurturing supportive ecosystems grounded in mutual respect and solidarity, women entrepreneurs cultivate an environment conducive to shared learning, mentorship, and collective advancement.

4. Championing Diversity and Inclusion

Diversity and inclusion are not merely buzzwords but fundamental principles driving innovation and growth in the modern business landscape. Women entrepreneurs are championing diversity across all facets of entrepreneurship, from leadership representation to product development and beyond. By embracing diverse perspectives, experiences, and talents, women entrepreneurs enrich their ventures, unlock new opportunities, and inspire meaningful change within their industries.

Conclusion

The journey of women entrepreneurs is a testament to resilience, resourcefulness, and unwavering determination in the face of adversity. Despite the challenges that loom large, women are seizing opportunities, shattering glass ceilings, and carving out their place in the entrepreneurial landscape. As we navigate the complexities of the modern world, let us champion inclusivity, cultivate empowerment, and forge a future where every woman's entrepreneurial aspirations can flourish, thrive, and inspire generations to come.

Chapter 3. Success Stories

Introduction

In the landscape of modern entrepreneurship, women are crafting their paths, breaking barriers, and redefining success on their terms. Their stories resonate with determination, resilience, and a passion for their craft. As we delve into the narratives of these remarkable women, we uncover tales of triumph, innovation, and unwavering dedication. Their journeys not only inspire but also serve as guiding lights for aspiring entrepreneurs, proving that with perseverance and vision, anything is possible. The success stories mentioned in this article belong to real individuals who have made significant contributions in their respective fields. Here's a brief overview of each individual mentioned:

Jane Chen: Co-founder of Embrace Innovations, Jane Chen developed a low-cost infant warmer to tackle infant mortality rates in developing countries.

Indra Nooyi: Former CEO of PepsiCo, Indra Nooyi broke stereotypes and redefined success in the corporate world through her strategic leadership.

Susan Wojcicki: Former CEO of YouTube, Susan Wojcicki played a crucial role in shaping the digital landscape and empowering creators worldwide.

Chanda Kochhar: Former CEO of ICICI Bank, Chanda Kochhar pioneered initiatives to provide banking services to rural communities, promoting financial inclusion.

Diane von Furstenberg: Fashion designer and founder of her eponymous label, Diane von Furstenberg is renowned for her iconic wrap dress and advocacy for female empowerment in the fashion industry.

Arianna Huffington: Co-founder of The Huffington Post, Arianna Huffington revolutionized online media and championed work-life balance and well-being.

Sara Blakely: Founder of Spanx, Sara Blakely disrupted the shapewear industry and inspired women to embrace confidence and authenticity.

These individuals have indeed made significant impacts in their respective domains and serve as inspirations for aspiring entrepreneurs around the world.

1. From Passion to Profit: The Story of Jane Chen

Jane Chen's journey embodies the spirit of turning adversity into opportunity. Co-founder of Embrace Innovations, Chen set out to tackle infant mortality rates in developing countries. Inspired by a Stanford University project, she developed a low-cost infant warmer, saving the lives of countless premature babies. Her dedication to social impact and innovative thinking underscores the power of entrepreneurship to effect meaningful change.

2. Breaking Glass Ceilings: The Rise of Indra Nooyi

Indra Nooyi's ascent to the summit of corporate leadership stands as a testament to perseverance and vision. As the former CEO of PepsiCo, Nooyi shattered stereotypes and redefined success in the corporate world. Her strategic acumen, coupled with a commitment to diversity and sustainability, propelled PepsiCo to new heights. Nooyi's journey inspires women to embrace leadership roles and challenge the status quo, paving the way for a more inclusive future.

3. Pioneering Tech Innovation: The Trailblazing Journey of Susan Wojcicki

Susan Wojcicki's transformative impact on the tech industry is nothing short of revolutionary. As the CEO of YouTube, Wojcicki played a pivotal role in shaping the digital landscape we navigate today. Her foresight and leadership propelled YouTube into a global phenomenon, empowering creators and revolutionizing content consumption. Wojcicki's journey underscores the importance of embracing innovation and fearlessly pursuing one's vision, regardless of the odds.

4. Empowering Communities: The Vision of Chanda Kochhar

Chanda Kochhar's story exemplifies the power of financial empowerment and inclusive growth. As the former CEO of ICICI Bank, Kochhar spearheaded initiatives to provide banking services to rural communities, transforming lives and livelihoods along the way. Her commitment to social responsibility and ethical leadership sets a precedent for driving sustainable change through corporate stewardship. Kochhar's journey serves as a reminder that true success lies in creating opportunities for others to thrive.

5. Redefining Fashion: The Evolution of Diane von Furstenberg

Diane von Furstenberg's indelible mark on the fashion industry transcends trends and seasons. As the founder of her eponymous fashion label, von Furstenberg pioneered the iconic wrap dress, symbolizing female empowerment and confidence. Her entrepreneurial spirit and creative vision continue to inspire generations of designers and fashion enthusiasts worldwide. Von Furstenberg's journey epitomizes the intersection of style and substance, proving that fashion can be a catalyst for self-expression and empowerment.

6. Navigating New Frontiers: The Odyssey of Arianna Huffington

Arianna Huffington's odyssey from journalism to digital media mogul exemplifies the transformative power of reinvention. As the co-founder of The Huffington Post, Huffington revolutionized the way we consume news and engage with online content. Her advocacy for work-life balance and holistic well-being underscores the importance of prioritizing personal wellness amidst professional success. Huffington's journey reminds us that true fulfillment stems from finding harmony in all aspects of life.

7. Disrupting Industries: The Bold Vision of Sara Blakely

Sara Blakely's journey from door-to-door saleswoman to self-made billionaire epitomizes the entrepreneurial spirit of resilience and innovation. As the founder of Spanx, Blakely revolutionized the shapewear industry, empowering women to feel confident and comfortable in their own skin. Her tenacity and ingenuity challenge conventional norms and redefine beauty standards, inspiring women to embrace authenticity and self-assurance. Blakely's story reaffirms the notion that with perseverance and belief in oneself, anything is achievable.

Conclusion

In the tapestry of women entrepreneurs, these stories weave a narrative of courage, determination, and unwavering resolve. From boardrooms to grassroots initiatives, these women are catalysts for change, driving innovation, and empowering communities. Their journeys serve as beacons of inspiration, illuminating the path for future generations of entrepreneurs to follow. As we celebrate their triumphs and milestones, let us remember that true success transcends mere accolades - it lies in the indelible mark we leave on the world and the lives we touch along the way.

Chapter 4. Leadership and Management Styles

Introduction

In the dynamic landscape of modern entrepreneurship, the role of women has been increasingly prominent and impactful. As women entrepreneurs navigate the complexities of the business world, they bring with them a diverse array of leadership and management styles. Understanding these styles not only illuminates the unique approaches women take to leadership but also offers valuable insights for aspiring entrepreneurs and business leaders alike.

Leadership and management are often used interchangeably, but they encompass distinct sets of skills and responsibilities. Leadership involves inspiring and guiding individuals toward a common vision, while management focuses on organizing resources and processes to achieve specific goals. Effective leadership and management are essential for the success and sustainability of any enterprise.

The Importance of Leadership and Management Styles

Leadership and management styles play a pivotal role in shaping organizational culture, driving innovation, and fostering employee engagement. By understanding and leveraging different styles, women entrepreneurs can adapt to diverse situations, motivate their teams, and navigate challenges effectively.

Transformational Leadership

Transformational leadership is characterized by visionary thinking, inspiration, and empowerment. Women entrepreneurs who adopt this style strive to create a shared vision and inspire their teams to exceed expectations. They prioritize mentorship, personal development, and fostering a supportive work environment. Transformational leaders empower their employees to innovate, take risks, and contribute creatively to the organization's goals.

Servant Leadership

Servant leadership revolves around the principle of serving others first. Women entrepreneurs embracing this style prioritize empathy, humility, and collaboration. They lead by example, demonstrating a genuine concern for the well-being and growth of their team members. Servant leaders actively listen to their employees, value their perspectives, and empower them to reach their full potential. By nurturing a culture of trust and reciprocity, they foster strong relationships and cultivate a sense of community within the organization.

Democratic Leadership

Democratic leadership emphasizes inclusivity, participation, and consensus-building. Women entrepreneurs who embrace this style value collective decision-making and seek input from all stakeholders. They encourage open communication, debate, and diversity of thought within their teams. Democratic leaders empower employees to voice their opinions, contribute ideas, and take ownership of the decision-making process. By fostering a culture of transparency and collaboration, they promote accountability and foster a sense of shared responsibility.

Transactional Leadership

Transactional leadership operates on the basis of rewards and punishments to motivate performance. Women entrepreneurs employing this style set clear expectations, establish performance metrics, and provide tangible incentives for goal achievement. They emphasize structure, efficiency, and adherence to established procedures. Transactional leaders utilize contingent rewards to reinforce desired behaviors and maintain organizational standards. While this approach can drive short-term results, its effectiveness may diminish in environments that require adaptability and innovation.

Charismatic Leadership

Charismatic leadership centers around the personal magnetism, charm, and persuasive communication of the leader. Women entrepreneurs embodying this style inspire trust, confidence, and loyalty through their charisma and compelling vision. They excel at articulating a compelling narrative, rallying support, and galvanizing their teams toward a common purpose. Charismatic leaders leverage their influence to inspire followership, overcome obstacles, and mobilize resources effectively.

Adaptive Leadership

Adaptive leadership emphasizes flexibility, resilience, and continuous learning in the face of uncertainty and change. Women entrepreneurs practicing this style embrace ambiguity, anticipate challenges, and adapt their strategies accordingly. They encourage experimentation, agility, and a willingness to challenge the status quo. Adaptive leaders empower their teams to navigate complexity, learn from failure, and pivot in response to evolving market dynamics. By fostering a culture of adaptability and innovation, they position their organizations for long-term success and sustainability.

Conclusion

In the dynamic landscape of entrepreneurship, women entrepreneurs bring a wealth of diverse perspectives, experiences, and approaches to leadership and management. By embracing a spectrum of styles - from transformational and servant leadership to democratic and adaptive leadership - women entrepreneurs can harness the full potential of their teams, drive innovation, and create sustainable value. Aspiring entrepreneurs and business leaders can draw inspiration from the rich tapestry of leadership styles exhibited by women entrepreneurs in the modern world, paving the way for inclusive, resilient, and purpose-driven organizations.

In conclusion, understanding different leadership and management styles adopted by women entrepreneurs is crucial for navigating the complexities of the modern business landscape. By embracing diverse approaches to leadership, women entrepreneurs can inspire, empower, and drive meaningful change within their organizations and beyond.

Chapter 5. Innovations and Disruptions

Introduction

Innovation refers to the creation or adoption of new ideas, products, processes, or services that bring about positive change or improvement. Disruption, on the other hand, involves the radical transformation or upheaval of established industries, markets, or practices through innovative approaches, often challenging existing norms and creating new opportunities. Both innovation and disruption are central to driving progress, growth, and competitiveness in various fields and industries.

In the dynamic landscape of entrepreneurship, women are emerging as powerful agents of change, driving innovation and disruption across various industries. Their contributions are reshaping economies, challenging traditional norms, and inspiring a new generation of leaders. In this article, we delve into the realm of innovations and disruptions spearheaded by women entrepreneurs, highlighting their transformative influence on the modern world.

Understanding Innovation

Innovation lies at the heart of entrepreneurship, propelling businesses towards growth and sustainability. Women entrepreneurs, equipped with diverse perspectives and experiences, bring a unique approach to innovation. Their ability to empathize, collaborate, and think creatively enables them to identify unmet needs and devise novel solutions.

1. Diversity and Creativity

Women entrepreneurs thrive in diverse environments, leveraging their multifaceted backgrounds to fuel creativity and innovation. By embracing inclusivity and fostering a culture of openness, they cultivate diverse teams that bring fresh insights and ideas to the table. This synergy of perspectives drives the innovation process, leading to the development of products and services that resonate with a broader audience.

2. Problem-solving and Resilience

In the face of challenges, women entrepreneurs exhibit remarkable resilience and adaptability. They approach problems as opportunities for innovation, applying strategic thinking and resourcefulness to overcome obstacles. By embracing failure as a stepping stone to success, they cultivate a culture of experimentation and learning within their organizations. This iterative process fuels innovation, allowing them to iterate rapidly and refine their offerings based on customer feedback.

Disrupting Industries

The rise of women entrepreneurs is disrupting traditional industries and challenging established norms, paving the way for transformative change. Their ventures span diverse sectors, from technology and finance to healthcare and education, revolutionizing established paradigms and driving industry-wide shifts.

1. Technology and Digital Transformation

Women entrepreneurs are at the forefront of the digital revolution, harnessing technology to create disruptive innovations that redefine business models and consumer experiences. From fintech startups (companies that leverage technology to deliver innovative financial products, services, and solutions) offering inclusive financial services to AI-driven platforms revolutionizing healthcare delivery, their ventures are reshaping the technological landscape. By leveraging *data analytics, machine learning*, and *blockchain technologies*, they are pioneering new frontiers and unlocking untapped opportunities in the digital economy.

Data analytics is the process of examining, cleansing, transforming, and interpreting large volumes of data to uncover meaningful insights, patterns, and trends that can inform decision-making, optimize processes, and drive business value. *Machine learning* is a branch of artificial intelligence enabling computers to learn from data and make predictions without explicit programming. *Blockchain technology* is a decentralized, immutable ledger system recording transactions across a network, known for its security and transparency.

2. Sustainable and Social Impact

Women entrepreneurs are championing sustainability and social impact, embedding purpose-driven principles into their business models. From eco-friendly fashion brands promoting ethical manufacturing practices to renewable energy startups advancing clean technologies, they are driving a paradigm shift towards responsible entrepreneurship. By aligning profit with purpose, they demonstrate that business success can coexist with social and environmental stewardship, inspiring a new generation of conscious consumers and investors.

Empowering Communities

Beyond economic prosperity, women entrepreneurs are empowering communities and driving inclusive growth. Their ventures create pathways to economic opportunity, particularly for marginalized groups, fostering entrepreneurship ecosystems that nurture talent and innovation.

1. Mentorship and Support Networks

Women entrepreneurs play a pivotal role in mentoring the next generation of leaders and fostering supportive networks that enable aspiring entrepreneurs to thrive. Through mentorship programs, networking events, and advocacy initiatives, they provide guidance, resources, and opportunities for professional development. By sharing their experiences and insights, they inspire confidence and resilience in emerging entrepreneurs, nurturing a culture of empowerment and collaboration.

2. Breaking Barriers and Shattering Stereotypes

Women entrepreneurs are breaking barriers and challenging stereotypes that have long constrained their participation in the entrepreneurial ecosystem. By leading by example and defying conventional norms, they pave the way for greater gender diversity and inclusion in entrepreneurship. Their achievements serve as a catalyst for change, dismantling systemic barriers and creating a more equitable playing field for future generations of women leaders.

Conclusion

Innovation and disruption are driving forces shaping the future of entrepreneurship, and women entrepreneurs are at the vanguard of this transformative journey. Through their ingenuity, resilience, and determination, they are redefining success, driving inclusive growth, and inspiring change across industries and communities. As we celebrate their achievements and contributions, let us continue to champion their cause and empower them to realize their full potential as catalysts for innovation and progress in the modern world.

Chapter 6. Tech and Digital Entrepreneurship

Introduction

In today's rapidly evolving landscape, the realms of technology and digital entrepreneurship stand as beacons of innovation, disruption, and endless possibilities. Within these spheres, women are not just participants; they are catalysts, shaping the future of business, technology, and society at large. As we delve into the intricate tapestry of women's roles in tech and digital sectors, it becomes evident that their prominence signifies not only progress but also the potential for profound transformation.

Unveiling Opportunities: Women Pioneering in Tech

The tech industry, once considered a predominantly male domain, has undergone a remarkable shift. Women are increasingly carving their niche in this dynamic sector, challenging stereotypes and redefining norms. From software engineering to artificial intelligence, women entrepreneurs are making significant strides, bringing fresh perspectives and innovative solutions to the table.

Breaking Barriers: Overcoming Challenges in Tech Entrepreneurship

Despite the progress, women in tech entrepreneurship encounter a myriad of challenges. Gender bias, unequal access to funding, and limited representation in leadership positions often hinder their advancement. However, these obstacles have fueled a collective resolve to shatter glass ceilings and foster an environment of inclusivity and empowerment.

The Digital Frontier: Women Driving Innovation

In the digital age, entrepreneurship transcends traditional boundaries, propelled by the boundless reach of the internet and digital technologies. Women entrepreneurs are leveraging these tools to revolutionize industries, disrupt conventional business models, and create unprecedented opportunities for growth and collaboration.

Embracing Disruption: Navigating the Digital Landscape

Digital entrepreneurship empowers women to unleash their creativity and pursue their entrepreneurial aspirations with unparalleled agility. From e-commerce ventures to digital marketing agencies, women-led enterprises are harnessing the power of technology to connect with global audiences, streamline operations, and drive sustainable growth.

Fostering Diversity: The Imperative of Inclusion

The emergence of women in tech and digital entrepreneurship underscores the importance of diversity and representation in the innovation ecosystem. By championing inclusivity and diversity, organizations can harness the full spectrum of talent, perspectives, and experiences, fostering creativity, resilience, and collective success.

Empowering the Next Generation: Cultivating Leadership and Mentorship

As trailblazers in their respective fields, women entrepreneurs play a pivotal role in inspiring and empowering the next generation of leaders. Through mentorship programs, networking initiatives, and advocacy efforts, they impart invaluable knowledge, guidance, and support, nurturing a culture of collaboration and empowerment.

Navigating the Future: Challenges and Opportunities Ahead

As we chart the course ahead, it is imperative to address the systemic barriers and inequities that persist in the tech and digital entrepreneurship landscape. By fostering inclusive policies, promoting equitable access to resources, and fostering a culture of mentorship and support, we can unlock the full potential of women entrepreneurs and drive collective innovation and prosperity.

Harnessing Technology for Social Impact

Beyond business success, women entrepreneurs are leveraging technology as a force for social good, driving meaningful change and addressing pressing global challenges. Whether it's advancing sustainability initiatives, promoting digital literacy, or advocating for social justice, women-led ventures are spearheading transformative initiatives that transcend borders and catalyze positive change.

Conclusion

In the tapestry of tech and digital entrepreneurship, women stand at the forefront, charting new horizons, and redefining the contours of possibility. Through resilience, determination, and innovation, they are reshaping industries, driving economic growth, and inspiring generations to come. As we embrace the limitless potential of women entrepreneurs, let us continue to champion diversity, foster inclusivity, and harness the power of technology to create a more equitable, prosperous, and sustainable future for all.

In the modern world of entrepreneurship, women are not just participants; they are architects of change, illuminating pathways to progress and prosperity in an ever-evolving landscape. As we celebrate their achievements and aspirations, let us embark on a collective journey of empowerment, innovation, and transformation, where every voice is heard, and every dream is within reach.

Chapter 7. Navigating Male-Dominated Industries

Introduction

In the dynamic landscape of entrepreneurship, women are breaking barriers and venturing into traditionally male-dominated industries with remarkable success. The journey, however, is not without its challenges. From technology to finance, engineering to construction, women entrepreneurs are carving their paths, reshaping industries, and inspiring generations to come. Navigating these male-dominated sectors demands resilience, innovation, and strategic maneuvering. In this article, we explore the strategies women entrepreneurs employ to thrive in such environments.

Innovations and Tech Entrepreneurship

Before delving into strategies for navigating male-dominated industries, it's essential to recognize the pivotal role of innovations and technology entrepreneurship in reshaping the business landscape. Technology has been a great equalizer, providing women with unprecedented opportunities to disrupt industries and challenge traditional norms.

Women entrepreneurs in tech are not only breaking stereotypes but also revolutionizing sectors once considered exclusive domains of men. From developing groundbreaking software to founding tech startups, women are at the forefront of innovation, driving change, and fostering inclusivity.

Tech entrepreneurship empowers women to leverage their creativity, expertise, and vision to address pressing societal needs while creating sustainable ventures. Through collaborative networks, mentorship programs, and access to resources, women in tech are not just navigating male-dominated industries but reshaping them altogether.

Strategies for Thriving in Male-Dominated Industries

1. Build a Strong Support Network

Surrounding oneself with mentors, allies, and peers who champion diversity and inclusion is crucial for success in male-dominated industries. Mentorship programs, networking events, and industry associations offer invaluable opportunities for women entrepreneurs to connect, learn, and grow.

2. Cultivate Confidence and Assertiveness

Confidence is key to navigating male-dominated industries. Women entrepreneurs must cultivate self-assurance, assertiveness, and resilience in the face of challenges and biases. Embracing one's expertise, vision, and accomplishments fosters credibility and command in professional settings.

3. Embrace Authentic Leadership

Authenticity is a powerful leadership trait that resonates across industries. Women entrepreneurs should embrace their unique perspectives, experiences, and leadership styles, fostering inclusive work environments that celebrate diversity and innovation.

4. Challenge Stereotypes and Bias

Addressing gender stereotypes and bias head-on is essential for fostering inclusive workplaces and driving systemic change. By challenging preconceived notions, advocating for diversity initiatives, and promoting equitable policies, women entrepreneurs can pave the way for greater representation and opportunities for future generations.

5. Focus on Results and Impact

In male-dominated industries, results speak volumes. Women entrepreneurs should focus on delivering exceptional outcomes, driving innovation, and creating tangible value for stakeholders. By showcasing their expertise, achievements, and contributions, women can position themselves as invaluable assets within their respective fields.

6. Invest in Continuous Learning and Skill Development

Lifelong learning is essential for navigating evolving industries and staying ahead of the curve. Women entrepreneurs should invest in continuous skill development, embrace emerging technologies, and seek opportunities for professional growth and advancement.

7. Forge Strategic Partnerships and Collaborations

Collaboration is key to success in male-dominated industries. Women entrepreneurs should forge strategic partnerships, alliances, and collaborations with industry leaders, organizations, and stakeholders. By leveraging collective expertise and resources, women can amplify their impact and drive meaningful change.

8. Lead by Example

As trailblazers in their fields, women entrepreneurs have a unique opportunity to lead by example and inspire future generations. By sharing their stories, advocating for inclusivity, and championing diversity, women can empower others to pursue their passions, break barriers, and redefine success on their own terms.

Conclusion

Navigating male-dominated industries requires vision, tenacity, and a steadfast commitment to driving change. Women entrepreneurs are not just challenging the status quo; they are reshaping industries, fostering innovation, and paving the way for a more inclusive and equitable future. By embracing strategic approaches, cultivating authentic leadership, and challenging societal norms, women entrepreneurs can thrive in traditionally male-dominated industries, leaving an indelible mark on the entrepreneurial landscape for generations to come.

Chapter 8. Building Support Networks

Introduction

In the dynamic landscape of entrepreneurship, women have been increasingly carving out their paths, overcoming challenges, and making significant strides in various industries. However, behind every successful woman entrepreneur lies a robust support network that plays a pivotal role in her journey. In this article, we delve into the significance of support networks for women entrepreneurs in the modern world, exploring how they navigate industry challenges, foster resilience, and thrive through collaboration.

The Landscape of Women Entrepreneurship

Women entrepreneurs today are venturing into diverse sectors, from technology and finance to healthcare and beyond. Despite facing systemic barriers and biases, women are breaking through glass ceilings, challenging stereotypes, and reshaping the entrepreneurial landscape. Their contributions to innovation, job creation, and economic growth are undeniable, highlighting the importance of fostering an inclusive and supportive environment for women in business.

Navigating Industry Challenges

In the competitive realm of entrepreneurship, women encounter a myriad of challenges ranging from access to funding and resources to gender-based discrimination and imposter syndrome. *Imposter syndrome* is a psychological phenomenon where individuals doubt their accomplishments, feel like frauds, and fear being exposed as incompetent despite evidence of their skills, achievements, and qualifications. The lack of representation in leadership positions, unequal opportunities, and limited access to networks further exacerbate these challenges, making it essential for women to seek out and build robust support systems.

The Power of Support Networks

Support networks serve as lifelines for women entrepreneurs, offering invaluable guidance, mentorship, and resources to navigate the complexities of business ownership. Whether through formal mentorship programs, peer-to-peer support groups, or online communities, these networks provide a safe space for women to share experiences, seek advice, and foster meaningful connections.

Mentorship and Guidance

Mentorship plays a pivotal role in the personal and professional development of women entrepreneurs. Having access to experienced mentors who understand the nuances of the industry can provide invaluable insights, guidance, and encouragement along the entrepreneurial journey. Mentorship not only helps women navigate challenges but also empowers them to set ambitious goals, overcome obstacles, and unlock their full potential.

Peer Support and Collaboration

Peer support networks offer women entrepreneurs the opportunity to connect with like-minded individuals facing similar challenges and aspirations. Through shared experiences, collaborative projects, and knowledge exchange, these networks foster a sense of camaraderie and solidarity among women in business. Collaborative initiatives such as co-working spaces, mastermind groups, and networking events create opportunities for women to leverage each other's strengths, resources, and networks for mutual benefit.

Building Resilience

Resilience is the cornerstone of success for women entrepreneurs navigating the ups and downs of entrepreneurship. In the face of setbacks, failures, and adversity, having a support network to lean on can make all the difference. By surrounding themselves with mentors, peers, and allies who believe in their vision and capabilities, women entrepreneurs can draw strength, resilience, and inspiration to persevere through challenges and emerge stronger than ever.

Overcoming Imposter Syndrome

Imposter syndrome, characterized by feelings of self-doubt and inadequacy, is a common challenge faced by women entrepreneurs as they strive for success. However, by fostering supportive relationships and cultivating a culture of empowerment, women can overcome imposter syndrome and embrace their unique talents, experiences, and achievements. Support networks provide a nurturing environment where women can celebrate their successes, share their vulnerabilities, and challenge self-limiting beliefs.

The Role of Intersectionality

It is essential to recognize that women entrepreneurs come from diverse backgrounds, experiences, and identities. Intersectionality, the interconnected nature of social categorizations such as race, ethnicity, class, and gender, shapes the experiences and challenges faced by women in entrepreneurship. Building inclusive support networks that acknowledge and celebrate intersectional identities is crucial for creating equitable opportunities and fostering a culture of belonging in the entrepreneurial ecosystem.

Embracing Diversity and Inclusion

Diversity and inclusion are not only moral imperatives but also strategic advantages for businesses and communities. By embracing diversity in their support networks, women entrepreneurs gain access to a wealth of perspectives, talents, and ideas that drive innovation and growth. Creating inclusive spaces where women from all walks of life feel valued, respected, and empowered is essential for building a vibrant and thriving entrepreneurial ecosystem.

Conclusion

In the journey of women entrepreneurship, building and nurturing support networks are paramount to success. By cultivating mentorship, fostering collaboration, and embracing diversity, women entrepreneurs can overcome challenges, amplify their impact, and pave the way for future generations of innovators and leaders. As we strive for a more equitable and inclusive world, let us continue to champion the power of support networks in empowering women entrepreneurs to thrive in the modern world.

Chapter 9. Balancing Work and Life

Introduction

In the modern entrepreneurial landscape, women are breaking barriers, shattering glass ceilings, and redefining success on their terms. However, amidst the pursuit of professional goals and entrepreneurial dreams, one critical aspect often gets overshadowed – achieving a harmonious balance between work and life. As women entrepreneurs navigate the complexities of business ownership, managing their personal lives alongside professional commitments becomes paramount. Understanding the dynamics of work-life balance, its challenges, and effective strategies is essential for sustaining well-being and fostering long-term success.

The Significance of Work-Life Balance

Work-life balance encompasses the equilibrium between professional responsibilities and personal pursuits, encompassing family, health, leisure, and personal development. For women entrepreneurs, achieving this balance is not merely a luxury but a necessity for holistic well-being. It allows them to thrive in both spheres, nurturing their businesses while nurturing themselves and their relationships.

Challenges Faced by Women Entrepreneurs

Women entrepreneurs encounter unique challenges in balancing work and life due to societal expectations, gender roles, and the relentless demands of entrepreneurship. Juggling multiple roles as business owners, caregivers, partners, and community members can lead to feelings of overwhelm, guilt, and burnout. Moreover, systemic barriers and biases in the business world often amplify these challenges, making it imperative for women to proactively address them.

Support Networks: Pillars of Strength

Central to achieving work-life balance are robust support networks comprising family, friends, mentors, and fellow entrepreneurs. These networks provide invaluable emotional support, guidance, and practical assistance, enabling women to navigate challenges with resilience and grace. Cultivating these relationships fosters a sense of community and solidarity, underscoring the power of collaboration in the entrepreneurial journey.

Strategies for Achieving Work-Life Balance

Achieving work-life balance requires intentional effort and strategic planning. Here are some effective strategies for women entrepreneurs to integrate into their lives.

1. Establish Boundaries: Define clear boundaries between work and personal time to prevent blurred lines and ensure dedicated periods for rest and rejuvenation. Communicate these boundaries with clients, employees, and stakeholders to foster mutual respect and understanding.

2. Prioritize Self-Care: Prioritize self-care practices that nurture physical, mental, and emotional well-being. Incorporate activities such as exercise, mindfulness, hobbies, and adequate sleep into daily routines to replenish energy levels and combat stress.

3. Delegate and Outsource: Delegate tasks within the business and leverage outsourcing opportunities to alleviate

workload burdens and focus on core competencies. Recognize the value of relinquishing control and empowering others to contribute to the success of the enterprise.

4. Embrace Flexibility: Embrace flexibility in work arrangements and adopt agile practices that accommodate personal commitments and unexpected challenges. Embracing remote work, flexible schedules, and technology-enabled solutions promotes autonomy and work-life integration.

5. Practice Time Management: Cultivate effective time management habits to optimize productivity and minimize distractions. Utilize tools such as calendars, to-do lists, and prioritization techniques to allocate time efficiently and achieve meaningful results.

6. Foster Work-Life Integration: Strive for a holistic approach to life where work and personal pursuits complement rather than compete with each other. Integrate moments of joy, fulfillment, and connection into both professional and personal endeavors to create a sense of harmony and fulfillment.

7. Cultivate Resilience: Cultivate resilience in the face of adversity by embracing setbacks as learning opportunities and reframing challenges as stepping stones to growth. Develop a resilient mindset grounded in optimism, adaptability, and self-compassion to navigate the ebbs and flows of the entrepreneurial journey.

Conclusion

In the dynamic landscape of entrepreneurship, achieving work-life balance is not a destination but a continuous journey of self-discovery and adaptation. For women entrepreneurs, it is a testament to their resilience, resourcefulness, and commitment to holistic well-being. By prioritizing self-care, fostering supportive networks, and embracing strategic practices, women can harmonize their professional aspirations with their personal lives, paving the way for sustainable success and fulfillment in the modern world of entrepreneurship. As they navigate the complexities of business ownership, let us champion their efforts and celebrate their resilience as they strive to strike a balance that honors both their ambitions and their essence as multifaceted individuals.

Chapter 10. Access to Capital

Introduction

In the modern landscape of entrepreneurship, access to capital stands as a cornerstone for success. However, despite strides in gender equality, women entrepreneurs still face significant challenges in accessing the financial resources necessary to start, sustain, and scale their businesses. This article delves into the complexities surrounding access to capital for women entrepreneurs, analyzing disparities, exploring funding sources, and highlighting the importance of support networks in leveling the playing field.

Understanding Disparities in Access to Capital

The disparity in access to capital for women entrepreneurs stems from a variety of systemic, cultural, and institutional factors. Historically, women have encountered obstacles in securing funding due to gender bias prevalent in financial institutions and venture capital firms. Studies reveal that female entrepreneurs receive a disproportionately small share of venture capital funding compared to their male counterparts. This bias often manifests in the form of unconscious stereotypes and preconceptions about the viability and potential of women-led businesses.

Moreover, women entrepreneurs frequently encounter challenges in accessing traditional forms of financing, such as bank loans, due to factors like limited collateral, credit history, and networks. Discriminatory lending practices and risk-averse attitudes further exacerbate these hurdles, hindering women from accessing the capital needed to turn their entrepreneurial visions into reality.

Exploring Funding Sources for Women Entrepreneurs

Despite the barriers, women entrepreneurs are increasingly turning to alternative funding sources to finance their ventures. One notable avenue is angel investing, where affluent individuals provide capital to startups in exchange for equity. Angel investor networks dedicated to supporting women-led businesses have emerged, offering mentorship, networking opportunities, and crucial funding to bridge the gender gap in entrepreneurship.

Crowdfunding platforms have also democratized access to capital by enabling entrepreneurs to raise funds from a diverse pool of investors online. Women entrepreneurs have leveraged crowdfunding to bypass traditional gatekeepers and garner support directly from their communities and beyond. These platforms not only provide financial resources but also serve as avenues for validation and market validation, empowering women to pursue their entrepreneurial aspirations.

Furthermore, government initiatives and grants aimed at supporting women-owned businesses play a pivotal role in facilitating access to capital. Programs offering financial assistance, technical support, and mentorship empower women entrepreneurs to overcome financial barriers and thrive in competitive markets. By fostering an ecosystem conducive to female entrepreneurship, policymakers and stakeholders contribute to economic growth, innovation, and social progress.

Challenges Faced by Women Entrepreneurs

Despite the availability of alternative funding sources, women entrepreneurs continue to encounter challenges on their entrepreneurial journey. The persistent gender gap in access to capital perpetuates inequalities in business ownership, growth, and wealth accumulation. Women-led startups often face higher scrutiny, tighter lending criteria, and lower valuation compared to their male counterparts, constraining their ability to scale and compete in the market.

Additionally, the intersectionality of gender with factors such as race, ethnicity, and socio-economic status exacerbates the challenges faced by marginalized women entrepreneurs. Women of color, LGBTQ+ women, and those from underprivileged backgrounds confront compounded barriers in accessing capital and resources, highlighting the need for intersectional approaches to address systemic inequities.

Support Networks and Strategies for Empowerment

In navigating the complex landscape of entrepreneurship, support networks emerge as catalysts for empowerment and success. Mentorship programs, incubators, and accelerators tailored to women entrepreneurs provide invaluable guidance, expertise, and connections essential for growth and resilience. By fostering a supportive ecosystem, these networks cultivate confidence, resilience, and a sense of belonging among women entrepreneurs, enabling them to thrive in male-dominated industries and markets.

Furthermore, initiatives aimed at promoting financial literacy and entrepreneurial skills empower women to navigate the intricacies of fundraising, investment, and financial management. By equipping women with the knowledge and tools to make informed financial decisions, these programs foster financial independence, resilience, and long-term sustainability in entrepreneurship.

Conclusion

Access to capital remains a critical determinant of success and opportunity for women entrepreneurs in the modern world. While disparities persist, the landscape is evolving with the emergence of alternative funding sources, supportive networks, and inclusive policies aimed at leveling the playing field. By addressing systemic barriers, challenging gender biases, and fostering a culture of inclusivity and empowerment, we can unlock the full potential of women entrepreneurs as drivers of innovation, growth, and social change in the global economy.

Introduction

Policy and advocacy involve efforts to influence decision-making processes and promote specific policies, laws, or initiatives to address social, political, or economic issues. This can include lobbying, public awareness campaigns, research, coalition-building, and engagement with policymakers, stakeholders, and the public to advocate for changes that align with particular goals or values. Policy and advocacy efforts aim to shape public opinion, mobilize support, and drive systemic change on a range of issues, from healthcare and education to environmental protection and human rights.

In the dynamic landscape of entrepreneurship, women have increasingly made significant strides, overcoming hurdles, and carving their paths in the modern business world. However, amidst their entrepreneurial journey, they often encounter systemic challenges that hinder their growth and potential. To address these challenges, policy initiatives and advocacy efforts play a pivotal role, shaping the environment in which women entrepreneurs operate. In this discourse, we delve into the realm of policy and advocacy, exploring its significance, challenges, and the transformative potential it holds for women entrepreneurs worldwide.

Understanding the Role of Policy Initiatives

Policy initiatives aimed at empowering women entrepreneurs are instrumental in fostering an environment conducive to their success. These initiatives encompass a spectrum of measures ranging from legislative reforms to targeted programs designed to address the unique needs and challenges faced by women in business.

1. Legislative Reforms

Legislative reforms serve as the cornerstone of policy interventions aimed at promoting gender equality and empowering women entrepreneurs. These reforms encompass a wide array of measures including anti-discrimination laws, equal pay legislation, and affirmative action policies that aim to level the playing field for women in business.

Such legislative reforms not only address overt discrimination but also seek to dismantle systemic barriers that impede women's access to resources, financing, and market opportunities. By enacting laws that promote gender parity and inclusivity, policymakers pave the way for women to thrive and succeed in the entrepreneurial landscape.

2. Access to Finance and Resources

One of the most significant challenges faced by women entrepreneurs is access to finance and resources. In many parts of the world, women encounter barriers when seeking funding for their ventures, with financial institutions exhibiting bias and reluctance to invest in women-led businesses.

Policy initiatives aimed at enhancing women's access to finance play a crucial role in addressing this disparity. Governments and international organizations have implemented various programs such as microfinance schemes, venture capital funds, and loan guarantee programs tailored to meet the needs of women entrepreneurs.

Additionally, initiatives aimed at providing women with access to resources such as mentorship, training, and networking opportunities are equally vital. By investing in capacity-building programs and entrepreneurship education, policymakers empower women with the skills and knowledge necessary to succeed in the competitive business landscape.

Advocacy Efforts: Amplifying Women's Voices

In addition to policy initiatives, advocacy efforts play a pivotal role in amplifying women's voices, driving awareness, and mobilizing support for gender-inclusive policies and practices. Advocacy efforts encompass a range of activities aimed at raising awareness, influencing public opinion, and mobilizing stakeholders to effect meaningful change.

1. Awareness Campaigns and Outreach

Awareness campaigns serve as a powerful tool for raising consciousness about the challenges faced by women entrepreneurs and the importance of gender-inclusive policies. Through targeted outreach initiatives, advocacy groups and non-profit organizations work to educate the public, policymakers, and business leaders about the value of gender diversity and the economic benefits of empowering women in business.

By spotlighting the achievements of women entrepreneurs and sharing their stories of resilience and success, advocacy campaigns seek to challenge stereotypes, inspire change, and foster a culture of inclusivity and empowerment.

2. Coalition Building and Collaborative Partnerships

Building coalitions and forging collaborative partnerships are essential strategies employed by advocacy groups to amplify their impact and drive systemic change. By bringing together diverse stakeholders including government agencies, civil society organizations, academia, and the private sector, advocacy groups leverage collective expertise and resources to advocate for policy reforms and institutional changes that benefit women entrepreneurs.

Through strategic alliances and partnerships, advocacy groups amplify their advocacy efforts, broaden their reach, and build momentum for change on a local, national, and global scale.

Challenges and Opportunities

While policy initiatives and advocacy efforts hold immense potential for advancing the interests of women entrepreneurs, they are not without challenges. In many contexts, entrenched gender norms, institutional biases, and political resistance pose formidable barriers to progress, impeding the implementation of gender-inclusive policies and hampering advocacy efforts.

1. Political Will and Leadership

The success of policy initiatives and advocacy efforts hinges on political will and leadership at the highest levels of government. Without strong commitment from policymakers and key stakeholders, efforts to promote gender equality and empower women entrepreneurs may falter, resulting in limited impact and systemic inertia.

Building political consensus and garnering support for gender-inclusive policies require sustained advocacy efforts and strategic engagement with policymakers, opinion leaders, and influencers across sectors.

2. Resource Constraints and Capacity Building

Advocacy groups and organizations advocating for women entrepreneurs often face resource constraints and capacity limitations, which hamper their ability to effectively mobilize support and drive change. Limited funding, staffing shortages, and competing priorities pose significant challenges, necessitating innovative approaches to resource mobilization and capacity building.

Investing in the capacity building of advocacy organizations, providing technical assistance, and fostering collaboration among stakeholders are essential strategies for strengthening the advocacy ecosystem and enhancing its impact.

Conclusion

Policy initiatives and advocacy efforts play a pivotal role in advancing the interests of women entrepreneurs, fostering an enabling environment for their success, and driving systemic change. By addressing systemic barriers, promoting gender equality, and amplifying women's voices, policymakers and advocates can unlock the full potential of women entrepreneurs, unleashing innovation, driving economic growth, and building a more inclusive and equitable society for all. As we continue to champion the cause of women entrepreneurs in the modern world, let us reaffirm our commitment to creating a future where every woman has the opportunity to thrive and succeed, unencumbered by systemic barriers or gender biases.

Chapter 12. Social Impact and Sustainability

Introduction

In the modern world, the role of women entrepreneurs transcends mere economic participation; it extends into realms of social impact and sustainability. As we navigate through the complexities of global challenges, women entrepreneurs emerge as formidable agents of change, driving initiatives that foster both social progress and environmental sustainability. This article delves into the multifaceted contributions of women entrepreneurs, exploring their role in policy and advocacy, as well as their broader impact on society and the environment.

Policy and Advocacy

Women entrepreneurs have long been at the forefront of policy and advocacy efforts, striving to create an enabling environment for business growth and social change. Through advocacy groups, lobbying efforts, and grassroots movements, they champion causes that promote gender equality, access to education, healthcare, and economic opportunities for women worldwide.

In recent years, we've witnessed significant strides in policy frameworks aimed at empowering women entrepreneurs. Initiatives such as gender-responsive budgeting, affirmative action programs, and gender mainstreaming policies have helped break down barriers and create pathways for women to thrive in entrepreneurial ventures. Moreover, the recognition of women's rights as human rights, as articulated in international conventions and agreements, has spurred governments and institutions to adopt gender-sensitive policies that support women's entrepreneurship.

The Role of Women Entrepreneurs in Driving Social Impact

Beyond policy and advocacy, women entrepreneurs play a pivotal role in driving tangible social impact within their communities and beyond. Their businesses often serve as catalysts for positive change, addressing pressing social issues and fostering inclusive development. From promoting education and healthcare to empowering marginalized groups and supporting local artisans, women-led enterprises embody a commitment to social responsibility and sustainable development.

One notable aspect of women's entrepreneurship is its emphasis on holistic approaches to community development. Many women entrepreneurs integrate social objectives into their business models, prioritizing ethical practices, fair labor standards, and community engagement. By harnessing the power of business as a force for good, they create sustainable solutions that uplift individuals and transform societies.

Education and Empowerment

Education lies at the heart of women's empowerment, serving as a cornerstone for economic independence and social mobility. Women entrepreneurs recognize the transformative power of education and actively invest in initiatives that expand access to learning opportunities for women and girls worldwide. Through scholarships, mentorship programs, and skills training initiatives, they equip aspiring entrepreneurs with the tools and knowledge needed to succeed in competitive markets.

Moreover, women entrepreneurs serve as role models and mentors, inspiring future generations of women to pursue their entrepreneurial ambitions. By sharing their stories of resilience, innovation, and success, they challenge traditional gender norms and redefine notions of leadership and entrepreneurship. In doing so, they pave the way for a more inclusive and diverse entrepreneurial ecosystem that celebrates women's contributions to economic and social progress.

Environmental Sustainability

In addition to driving social impact, women entrepreneurs are increasingly recognized for their role in promoting environmental sustainability. As stewards of the planet, they recognize the urgent need to address environmental challenges and mitigate the impact of climate change. From eco-friendly manufacturing practices to sustainable supply chain management, women-led enterprises embrace innovative solutions that prioritize environmental conservation and resource efficiency.

Furthermore, women entrepreneurs are instrumental in advancing the transition towards a green economy, characterized by low-carbon technologies, renewable energy sources, and circular business models. Through eco-conscious initiatives and eco-entrepreneurship ventures, they demonstrate the feasibility of sustainable business practices while advocating for policies that incentivize environmental stewardship.

Collaboration and Collective Action

Collaboration lies at the heart of effective social impact and sustainability efforts. Women entrepreneurs recognize the power of collective action and actively seek partnerships with governments, civil society organizations, and private sector stakeholders to amplify their impact. By forging strategic alliances and leveraging collective resources, they catalyze transformative change on a global scale, addressing systemic challenges and driving sustainable development outcomes.

Moreover, women's networks and entrepreneurship ecosystems serve as incubators for innovation and collaboration, providing platforms for knowledge exchange, capacity building, and peer support. Through networking events, workshops, and forums, women entrepreneurs share best practices, explore new business opportunities, and forge meaningful connections that transcend geographical boundaries and cultural barriers.

Conclusion

Women entrepreneurs are indispensable agents of change, driving social impact and sustainability through their innovative ventures and visionary leadership. From advocating for policy reforms to championing environmental conservation, they embody the principles of social responsibility, inclusivity, and sustainability in their business practices. As we strive towards a more equitable and sustainable future, harnessing the full potential of women entrepreneurs is essential for creating a world where prosperity, opportunity, and well-being are accessible to all.

Through collaboration, empowerment, and collective action, women entrepreneurs are reshaping the entrepreneurial landscape, driving positive change that transcends borders and transforms lives. As we celebrate their achievements and contributions, let us reaffirm our commitment to supporting and empowering women entrepreneurs as catalysts for a brighter, more sustainable tomorrow.

Chapter 13. Global Perspectives

Introduction

In the ever-evolving landscape of entrepreneurship, women around the globe are making significant strides, challenging stereotypes, and reshaping economies. Their journeys are as diverse as the cultures and societies they represent. From Silicon Valley to rural villages in developing countries, women entrepreneurs are leaving an indelible mark on the business world. In this article, we explore the global perspectives of women entrepreneurs, delving into their experiences across different countries and cultures, and examining the social impact and sustainability initiatives they champion.

Diverse Experiences: A Global Overview

The experiences of women entrepreneurs vary significantly depending on the socio-cultural and economic contexts of their respective countries. In developed nations like the United States, women have increasingly broken into traditionally male-dominated industries, founding tech startups, leading financial institutions, and launching innovative ventures across diverse sectors. Silicon Valley, often hailed as the epicenter of innovation, has seen a surge in female-led startups, challenging the status quo and redefining success criteria.

Conversely, in many developing countries, women face a myriad of challenges in pursuing entrepreneurial endeavors. Cultural norms, limited access to education and resources, and systemic barriers often hinder their progress. Despite these obstacles, women in countries like India, Nigeria, and Bangladesh are carving out niches for themselves, leveraging their creativity, resilience, and community support to establish thriving businesses.

Experiences in Different Countries and Cultures

India: In India, a country known for its rich tapestry of cultures and traditions, women entrepreneurs are driving change across diverse industries. From leading technology firms to pioneering social enterprises, Indian women are at the forefront of innovation. Initiatives such as the Women Entrepreneurship Platform (WEP) have provided a platform for aspiring female entrepreneurs to connect, collaborate, and access resources. However, challenges such as gender bias, lack of access to finance, and limited market opportunities persist, underscoring the need for targeted interventions and policy reforms.

Nigeria: In Nigeria, women entrepreneurs play a vital role in driving economic growth and development. From the bustling markets of Lagos to the tech hubs of Abuja, Nigerian women are harnessing the power of entrepreneurship to create jobs, empower communities, and foster inclusive growth. Organizations like the She Leads Africa accelerator program provide mentorship, training, and funding opportunities for aspiring female entrepreneurs, enabling them to overcome barriers and scale their ventures. Despite facing systemic challenges such as infrastructure deficits and regulatory hurdles, Nigerian women continue to defy odds and thrive in the entrepreneurial landscape.

Sweden: In Sweden, a country known for its progressive policies and gender equality initiatives, women entrepreneurs enjoy relatively favorable conditions compared to many other nations. With robust support systems, access to affordable childcare, and a culture of innovation, Swedish women are increasingly venturing into entrepreneurship, driving innovation and sustainable development. Initiatives like the Swedish Innovation Agency (Vinnova) provide funding and support for startups led by women, fostering a conducive ecosystem for female entrepreneurship to flourish. However, disparities still exist, particularly in male-dominated sectors such as technology and finance, highlighting the need for continued efforts to promote gender diversity and inclusion.

Social Impact and Sustainability Initiatives

Beyond economic success, women entrepreneurs are increasingly prioritizing social impact and sustainability in their business ventures. From promoting ethical sourcing and environmental conservation to championing gender equality and community development, women-led enterprises are driving positive change on a global scale.

In Kenya, organizations like EcoPost, founded by entrepreneur Lorna Rutto, are tackling environmental challenges by producing eco-friendly charcoal briquettes from recycled agricultural waste. Not only does this initiative reduce deforestation and air pollution, but it also creates employment opportunities for local women, empowering them economically and socially.

Similarly, in Brazil, social enterprises like Rede Asta are empowering marginalized women by providing training in artisanal crafts and connecting them with market opportunities. By promoting fair trade practices and empowering women to become financially independent, Rede Asta is transforming lives and communities across Brazil.

Conclusion

Women entrepreneurs are a driving force for innovation, growth, and social change in the modern world. Their experiences, shaped by diverse cultural contexts and socio-economic realities, offer valuable insights into the challenges and opportunities facing female entrepreneurs globally. By fostering an enabling environment, promoting gender equality, and investing in women's entrepreneurship, societies can unlock the full potential of women as catalysts for sustainable development and inclusive prosperity. As we celebrate the achievements of women entrepreneurs around the world, let us continue to support and empower them on their journey towards a more equitable and prosperous future.

Chapter 14. Overcoming Impostor Syndrome

Introduction

In the realm of entrepreneurship, women have been increasingly making their mark, breaking barriers, and reshaping industries. Their journeys are often filled with triumphs, challenges, and moments of self-doubt. One such challenge that many women entrepreneurs face is impostor syndrome, a phenomenon where individuals doubt their accomplishments and have a persistent fear of being exposed as a fraud. In this article, we explore the nuances of impostor syndrome, its impact on women entrepreneurs, and strategies to overcome it, drawing insights from personal stories and experiences.

Understanding Impostor Syndrome

Impostor syndrome is not exclusive to women entrepreneurs, but its prevalence and manifestation in this demographic are noteworthy. Despite achieving success and recognition, many women entrepreneurs experience feelings of inadequacy and self-doubt. They may attribute their accomplishments to luck or external factors rather than acknowledging their skills and hard work. This phenomenon can be attributed to societal expectations, cultural norms, and personal experiences that shape one's perception of success and competence.

The Impact of Impostor Syndrome

Impostor syndrome can have profound effects on women entrepreneurs, both personally and professionally. It can hinder their ability to take risks, pursue new opportunities, and step into leadership roles. The fear of failure and being exposed as a fraud can lead to self-sabotage and limit their potential for growth. Moreover, impostor syndrome can contribute to stress, anxiety, and burnout, affecting overall well-being and fulfillment.

Personal Struggles and Growth

Many successful women entrepreneurs have grappled with impostor syndrome throughout their careers. Take, for example, Sarah, the founder of a tech startup, who constantly questioned her abilities despite securing funding and expanding her business. She felt like she didn't belong in the male-dominated tech industry and feared being perceived as incompetent. However, through introspection and support from mentors and peers, Sarah gradually embraced her accomplishments and silenced her inner critic.

Strategies for Overcoming Impostor Syndrome

1. Acknowledge Your Achievements: Take stock of your accomplishments and recognize the hard work and dedication that have brought you to where you are today. Keep a journal of your successes, both big and small, to remind yourself of your capabilities.

2. Challenge Negative Thoughts: When feelings of self-doubt arise, challenge them with evidence of your competence and past achievements. Reframe negative thoughts into positive affirmations and cultivate a growth mindset that focuses on learning and improvement.

3. Seek Support and Mentorship: Surround yourself with a network of supportive mentors, peers, and colleagues who

can offer guidance, encouragement, and perspective. Share your experiences with trusted individuals who understand the challenges of entrepreneurship.

4. Embrace Vulnerability: Recognize that vulnerability is not a sign of weakness but rather a catalyst for growth and connection. Share your struggles and insecurities openly, both with yourself and with others, fostering authenticity and resilience.

5. Practice Self-Compassion: Treat yourself with kindness and compassion, especially during moments of self-doubt and failure. Practice self-care activities that nourish your mind, body, and spirit, allowing yourself grace and acceptance.

6. Set Realistic Goals: Break down your goals into manageable steps and celebrate progress along the way. Focus on continuous improvement rather than perfection, embracing the journey of entrepreneurship with resilience and determination.

Conclusion

Impostor syndrome is a common yet often overlooked challenge that many women entrepreneurs face in their pursuit of success. By understanding its origins, acknowledging its impact, and implementing strategies for self-awareness and growth, women can overcome impostor syndrome and thrive in their entrepreneurial endeavors. Remember, you are not alone in your journey, and your worth is not defined by external validation. Embrace your unique strengths, cultivate resilience, and let your brilliance shine in the modern world of entrepreneurship.

Chapter 15. Failure and Resilience

Introduction

In the ever-evolving landscape of entrepreneurship, the journey is paved with triumphs, setbacks, and the enduring resilience required to navigate through them. For women entrepreneurs in the modern world, the path to success often intersects with the harsh reality of failure. Yet, it is within the depths of failure that resilience is forged, transforming setbacks into stepping stones towards growth and achievement.

Understanding Failure: The Impostor Syndrome

1. The Impostor Syndrome Phenomenon

One of the most pervasive challenges faced by women entrepreneurs is the impostor syndrome. This psychological phenomenon engulfs individuals, making them doubt their accomplishments and fear being exposed as frauds, despite evident competence and success. Women, especially in male-dominated industries, often grapple with feelings of inadequacy and self-doubt, attributing their achievements to luck rather than merit.

2. Navigating Self-Doubt and External Pressures

The pressure to excel in a competitive business environment exacerbates the internal turmoil of self-doubt. Women entrepreneurs often face heightened scrutiny and skepticism, amplifying the burden of proving themselves capable. The fear of failure looms large, casting shadows of uncertainty on their entrepreneurial journey.

3. Embracing Vulnerability as Strength

Acknowledging vulnerability is the first step towards conquering the impostor syndrome. Women entrepreneurs must recognize that vulnerability does not equate to weakness; rather, it signifies courage and authenticity. By embracing vulnerability, entrepreneurs empower themselves to confront their fears and confront the challenges with resilience.

Learning from Setbacks: The Path to Growth

1. Embracing Failure as a Catalyst for Growth

Failure is an inevitable facet of the entrepreneurial voyage. Instead of viewing setbacks as insurmountable obstacles, women entrepreneurs can reframe failure as a catalyst for growth. Each setback presents an invaluable opportunity for reflection, learning, and adaptation.

2. Cultivating a Growth Mindset

Central to overcoming failure is cultivating a growth mindset - a belief that abilities and intelligence can be developed through dedication and hard work. Women entrepreneurs must embrace challenges with optimism, viewing obstacles as temporary roadblocks on the journey to success. By reframing setbacks as learning experiences, entrepreneurs foster resilience and perseverance.

3. Fostering a Culture of Innovation and Adaptability

Innovation thrives in environments that embrace experimentation and risk-taking. Women entrepreneurs must foster a culture that celebrates creativity and resilience, encouraging team members to explore new ideas and solutions. By promoting adaptability, entrepreneurs equip themselves with the agility to navigate through dynamic market landscapes.

Building Resilience: The Foundation of Success

1. Cultivating Emotional Intelligence

Emotional intelligence forms the cornerstone of resilience, enabling women entrepreneurs to navigate through adversity with grace and composure. By cultivating self-awareness and empathy, entrepreneurs foster meaningful connections and collaborations, fostering a supportive ecosystem of growth and innovation.

2. Seeking Mentorship and Support Networks

The journey of entrepreneurship can be solitary, but it does not have to be lonely. Women entrepreneurs must proactively seek mentorship and cultivate support networks comprising like-minded individuals and industry peers. Through mentorship, entrepreneurs gain invaluable insights, guidance, and encouragement, bolstering their resilience and resolve.

3. Prioritizing Self-Care and Well-Being

Amidst the demands of entrepreneurship, prioritizing self-care and well-being is paramount. Women entrepreneurs must recognize the importance of balance and nourish their physical, mental, and emotional health. By prioritizing self-care, entrepreneurs replenish their energy reserves, fortifying themselves to confront challenges with resilience and vitality.

Conclusion

In the tapestry of entrepreneurship, failure and resilience are intertwined threads that weave the fabric of success. For women entrepreneurs in the modern world, the journey is fraught with obstacles and uncertainties, yet it is also brimming with boundless opportunities and potential.

By confronting the impostor syndrome, learning from setbacks, and cultivating resilience, women entrepreneurs emerge as architects of their destiny, forging pathways of innovation, empowerment, and transformation. In the face of adversity, they stand undaunted, guided by the unwavering belief that within every setback lies the seed of resilience, ready to blossom into the fruits of triumph and fulfillment.

Chapter 16. The Future of Women Entrepreneurship

Introduction

As we delve into the intricate world of women entrepreneurship, navigating through historical perspectives, challenges, success stories, and innovations, we arrive at a pivotal juncture: contemplating the future of women in entrepreneurship. This final chapter serves not only as a culmination of the insights gathered but also as a beacon illuminating the path forward for aspiring and current women entrepreneurs in the modern world.

Embracing Evolutionary Trends

The journey of women in entrepreneurship has been one of resilience, determination, and evolution. From humble beginnings where societal norms often dictated their roles, women entrepreneurs have shattered glass ceilings and rewritten narratives. Looking ahead, the trajectory continues to ascend, propelled by a confluence of factors including technological advancements, shifting cultural paradigms, and an increasingly interconnected global landscape.

Embracing Technology and Digital Transformation

One of the most profound shifts shaping the future of women entrepreneurship lies in the realm of technology and digital innovation. As digitalization permeates every facet of our lives, women entrepreneurs are harnessing its transformative power to disrupt industries, redefine business models, and reach unprecedented markets.

Whether it's leveraging artificial intelligence, blockchain, or e-commerce platforms, technology serves as an enabler, leveling the playing field and opening doors to new possibilities.

Cultivating Leadership and Management Excellence

In the landscape of tomorrow, leadership and management styles will undergo continual evolution, reflecting the diverse perspectives and experiences of women entrepreneurs. Collaborative leadership, empathetic management, and a commitment to diversity and inclusion will emerge as cornerstones of success. As women assume leadership roles across industries, their ability to foster innovation, cultivate talent, and drive organizational change will redefine notions of effective leadership in the entrepreneurial landscape.

Navigating Complex Ecosystems

Despite significant strides, women entrepreneurs continue to navigate complex ecosystems characterized by gender biases, funding disparities, and institutional barriers. However, the future heralds a paradigm shift - a collective endeavor to dismantle systemic inequities and foster inclusive environments conducive to female entrepreneurship. Initiatives aimed at promoting gender diversity in venture capital, advocating for equitable policies, and amplifying women's voices in decision-making forums will pave the way for a more inclusive entrepreneurial ecosystem.

Fostering Collaboration and Support Networks

As women entrepreneurs chart their course in uncharted waters, the importance of collaboration and support networks cannot be overstated. Building upon the foundation of mentorship, peer support, and strategic alliances, women entrepreneurs will cultivate robust ecosystems of mutual empowerment and growth. From co-working spaces to virtual communities, these networks serve as catalysts for innovation, resilience, and collective progress.

Embracing Diversity and Inclusion

The future of women entrepreneurship is inherently intertwined with the principles of diversity, equity, and inclusion. Embracing diverse perspectives, championing underrepresented voices, and fostering cultures of belonging will fuel innovation, drive economic growth, and shape a more equitable future. By transcending boundaries of gender, ethnicity, and background, women entrepreneurs will redefine the entrepreneurial landscape, unleashing untapped potential and creating pathways for shared prosperity.

Harnessing the Power of Social Impact

Beyond profit margins and market share, the future of women entrepreneurship lies in its capacity to effect positive social change. From sustainable business practices to community empowerment initiatives, women entrepreneurs are at the forefront of driving meaningful impact across local and global communities. As consumers increasingly gravitate towards socially conscious brands, the intersection of business and social good becomes not only a moral imperative but also a strategic advantage.

Embracing Uncertainty with Resilience

In an era characterized by rapid change and uncertainty, resilience emerges as a defining trait of women entrepreneurs. Embracing failure as a catalyst for growth, adapting to dynamic market forces, and embracing ambiguity with courage and conviction will be essential skills in the entrepreneurial toolkit. By cultivating resilience in the face of adversity, women entrepreneurs will navigate turbulent waters with grace, perseverance, and an unwavering commitment to their vision.

Charting a Bold Path Forward

As we reflect on the past, embrace the present, and envision the future of women entrepreneurship, one thing remains abundantly clear: the journey ahead is as promising as it is challenging. By harnessing the power of technology, fostering inclusive ecosystems, embracing diversity and social impact, and cultivating resilience in the face of uncertainty, women entrepreneurs are poised to redefine the entrepreneurial landscape for generations to come.

In closing, the future of women entrepreneurship is not merely a destination to be reached but a journey to be embraced - one characterized by possibility, perseverance, and boundless potential. As we embark on this transformative odyssey, let us draw inspiration from the trailblazers who have come before us, leverage the lessons learned along the way, and chart a bold path forward towards a future where every woman has the opportunity to realize her entrepreneurial dreams.

"Women Entrepreneurs in the Modern World" delves into the dynamic landscape of female entrepreneurship through a comprehensive lens. From tracing historical trajectories in Chapter 1 to envisioning the future in Chapter 16, this book navigates the multifaceted journey of women in business. Each chapter, meticulously structured, encapsulates pivotal themes such as challenges, success stories, leadership styles, innovations, and global perspectives. From dissecting tech entrepreneurship to confronting imposter syndrome, the book explores the nuances of female entrepreneurship with depth and insight. With an emphasis on resilience, collaboration, and social impact, "Women Entrepreneurs in the Modern World" not only celebrates the triumphs but also addresses the systemic barriers that women entrepreneurs encounter, offering a roadmap for empowerment and change in the entrepreneurial landscape.

ABOUT THE AUTHOR

Mr. C. P. Kumar is a retired Scientist 'G' from National Institute of Hydrology, Roorkee, Uttarakhand, India. He is also a Reiki Healer and Chakra Balancing practitioner (with pendulum dowsing) and offers Emotional Freedom Technique (EFT) to help individuals with emotional issues. Mr. Kumar has authored many books on technical, spiritual, and social topics.

For further details, you may visit his webpage
https://www.angelfire.com/nh/cpkumar/virgo.html

www.ingramcontent.com/pod-product-compliance
Lightning Source LLC
Chambersburg PA
CBHW070945290526
45795CB00005B/1646